RAMADAN
Revival
JOURNAL

PLAN YOUR FAST
DESIGN YOUR DAY
REVIVE YOUR RAMADAN

Name ....

Email ....

Phone ....

Year ....

Title:　　　　Ramadan Revival Journal
Proofreading:　Wordsmith

ISBN: 978-1-952306-11-2

FIRST EDITION | FEBRUARY 2021

إِنَّمَا الْأَعْمَالُ بِالنِّيَّاتِ

*"Actions are
according to intentions…"*

RELATED BY BUKHARI & MUSLIM

Plan your entire day around your salah. Once your day is planned out, make it happen! This is about becoming more intentional with your time and spending it wisely.

A daily prayer to reflect on.

RAMADAN

DATE *April 12, 2021*

Did I fast? X

"Then which of your Lord's favors will you both deny?" 55:16

We all have much to be thankful for. Gratitude opens our spiritual eyes.

This Ramadan, let's make it a habit to read from the Quran daily. Keep track of what you've read and share a personal reflection here.

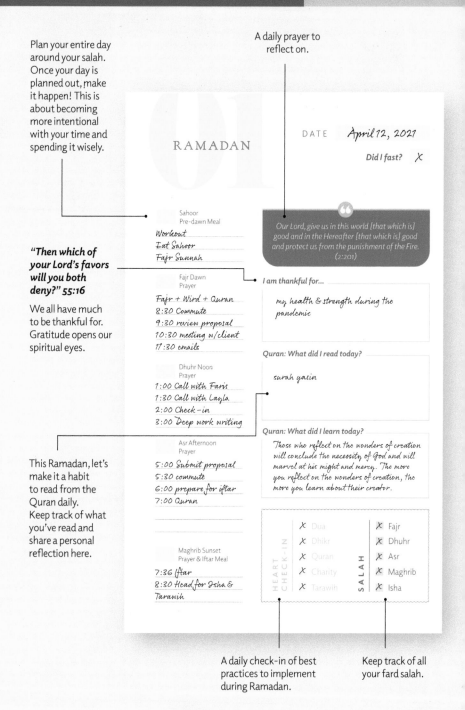

Sahoor
Pre-dawn Meal

Workout
Eat Sahoor
Fajr Sunnah

Fajr Dawn
Prayer

Fajr + Wird + Quran
8:30 Commute
9:30 review proposal
10:30 meeting w/client
11:30 emails

Dhuhr Noon
Prayer

1:00 Call with Faris
1:30 Call with Layla
2:00 Check-in
3:00 Deep work writing

Asr Afternoon
Prayer

5:00 Submit proposal
5:30 commute
6:00 prepare for iftar
7:00 Quran

Maghrib Sunset
Prayer & Iftar Meal

7:36 Iftar
8:30 Head for Isha &
Tarawih

Our Lord, give us in this world [that which is] good and in the Hereafter [that which is] good and protect us from the punishment of the Fire. (2:201)

I am thankful for...

my health & strength during the pandemic

Quran: What did I read today?

surah yasin

Quran: What did I learn today?

Those who reflect on the wonders of creation will conclude the necessity of God and will marvel at his might and mercy. The more you reflect on the wonders of creation, the more you learn about their creator.

HEART CHECK-IN		SALAH	
X	Dua	X	Fajr
X	Dhikr	X	Dhuhr
X	Quran	X	Asr
X	Charity	X	Maghrib
X	Tarawih	X	Isha

A daily check-in of best practices to implement during Ramadan.

Keep track of all your fard salah.

Your most important to-dos.

What would you like your three biggest wins for the day to be? This is a space to list your targets.

Intentional Duas

How often do you want to make heartfelt dua, but you sit there struggling to covey your thoughts and emotions to Allah?

This is a space where everyday you'll add a few prayers to the list. The natural result of this is an intimate conversation between you and Allah in *draft* mode sort of speak. This will help you make a more meaningful and intentional dua this Ramadan.

IMPORTANT TASKS FOR TODAY

1) Call 5 leads

2) 1 hour of writing

3) Catch up on all emails!

Duas
TO MAKE

Ya Raab, make me sincere in my duas.

Ya Allah, assist us with physical & emotional strength to be a good parent & example for our children.

Ya Allah invite me to Makkah and Madinah this year.

Ya Allah keep us safe and healthy, at all times.

GOOD DEEDS FOR TODAY

1) Support Imam Ghazali Institute's Riyad al-Salihin Launch Good

2) Pray all my sunnahs today!

3) Compliment someone with sincerity!

Daily Reflections

Part of reflecting is looking at what one has sent on ahead.

Self-reflection can help you process your thoughts and feelings. When we keep our thoughts floating around in our heads, we only confuse or frustrate ourselves more. Getting your thoughts on paper can help you understand.

IMPORTANT TASKS FOR TOMORROW

1) Finish next week's blog

2) Draft of event overview

3) Write proposal for Abdulla

Daily
REFLECTIONS

Making duas on the spot in english is a lot harder. Today, I tried making dua intentionally, for 10 mins. It's harder than it seems... and I need to work on that this Ramadan.

Bismillah...

3 Good Deeds

Ramadan is a month where the reward for good deeds are multiplied. Let's make every moment count!

Thinking Ahead

This is an opportunity to think ahead and prepare for tomorrow.

Ramadan **in Focus**

✓	#	GOAL STATEMENT / WRITE YOUR RAMADAN GOALS HERE

1	2	3
6	7	8
11	12	13
16	17	18
21	22	23
26	27	28

4	5

9	10

14	15

19	20

24	25

29	30

MAJOR GOALS

_____
_____
_____
_____
_____
_____
_____
_____
_____
_____
_____
_____
_____
_____
_____
_____
_____
_____
_____
_____
_____
_____

How to Complete a Recital of the Complete Quran this Ramadan

	FAJR	DHUHR	ASR	MAGHRIB	'ISHA
1 Complete Recitation	4	4	4	4	4
2 Complete Recitation	8	8	8	8	8
3 Complete Recitation	12	12	12	12	12
4 Complete Recitation	16	16	16	16	16

By reciting a minimum of 4 pages before or after each prayer, you will, by the permission and grace of Allah, complete the recital of the complete Quran this Ramadan*.

*Based on the 604-page mushaf print.

01

DATE

Did I fast?

Sahoor
Pre-dawn Meal

> *Our Lord, give us good in this world, and good in the Hereafter; protect us from the punishment of the Fire. (2:201)*

Fajr Dawn
Prayer

I am thankful for...

Dhuhr Noon
Prayer

Quran: What did I read today?

Quran: What did I learn today?

Asr Afternoon
Prayer

Maghrib Sunset
Prayer & Iftar Meal

HEART CHECK-IN

Dua
Dhikr
Quran
Charity
Tarawih

SALAH

Fajr
Dhuhr
Asr
Maghrib
Isha

IMPORTANT TASKS
FOR TODAY

1)

2)

3)

GOOD DEEDS
FOR TODAY

1)

2)

3)

IMPORTANT TASKS
FOR TOMORROW

1)

2)

3)

Duas TO MAKE

Daily REFLECTIONS

RAMADAN

Did I fast?

Sahoor
Pre-dawn Meal

> *Our Lord, pour upon us patience and plant firmly our feet and give us victory over the disbelieving people. (2:250)*

Fajr Dawn
Prayer

I am thankful for...

Dhuhr Noon
Prayer

Quran: What did I read today?

Asr Afternoon
Prayer

Quran: What did I learn today?

Maghrib Sunset
Prayer & Iftar Meal

HEART CHECK-IN		SALAH	
	Dua		Fajr
	Dhikr		Dhuhr
	Quran		Asr
	Charity		Maghrib
	Tarawih		Isha

**IMPORTANT TASKS
FOR TODAY**

1)

2)

3)

Duas
TO MAKE

**GOOD DEEDS
FOR TODAY**

1)

2)

3)

Daily
REFLECTIONS

**IMPORTANT TASKS
FOR TOMORROW**

1)

2)

3)

DHIKR

SubhanAllah (33 times)
Glory be to God

Alhamdulillah (33 times)
Praise be to God

Allahu Akbar (34 times)
God is Greater

سبحان الله

الحمد لله

الله أكبر

RAMADAN

DATE

Did I fast?

Sahoor
Pre-dawn Meal

> *Our Lord, do not impose blame upon us if we have forgotten or erred. (2:286)*

Fajr Dawn
Prayer

I am thankful for...

Dhuhr Noon
Prayer

Quran: What did I read today?

Asr Afternoon
Prayer

Quran: What did I learn today?

Maghrib Sunset
Prayer & Iftar Meal

HEART CHECK-IN
- Dua
- Dhikr
- Quran
- Charity
- Tarawih

SALAH
- Fajr
- Dhuhr
- Asr
- Maghrib
- Isha

**IMPORTANT TASKS
FOR TODAY**

1)

2)

3)

**GOOD DEEDS
FOR TODAY**

1)

2)

3)

**IMPORTANT TASKS
FOR TOMORROW**

1)

2)

3)

RAMADAN

Did I fast?

Sahoor
Pre-dawn Meal

....

....

....

> "
>
> *Our Lord, lay not upon us a burden like that which You laid upon those before us. (2:286)*

Fajr Dawn
Prayer

....

....

....

....

I am thankful for...

Dhuhr Noon
Prayer

....

....

....

Quran: What did I read today?

Asr Afternoon
Prayer

....

....

....

....

Quran: What did I learn today?

Maghrib Sunset
Prayer & Iftar Meal

....

....

HEART CHECK-IN		SALAH	
	Dua		Fajr
	Dhikr		Dhuhr
	Quran		Asr
	Charity		Maghrib
	Tarawih		Isha

**IMPORTANT TASKS
FOR TODAY**

1)

2)

3)

**GOOD DEEDS
FOR TODAY**

1)

2)

3)

**IMPORTANT TASKS
FOR TOMORROW**

1)

2)

3)

DATE

Did I fast?

Sahoor
Pre-dawn Meal

> *Our Lord, burden us not with that which we have no ability to bear. And pardon us; and forgive us; and have mercy upon us. You are our protector, so give us victory over the disbelieving people. (2:286)*

Fajr Dawn
Prayer

I am thankful for...

Quran: What did I read today?

Dhuhr Noon
Prayer

Quran: What did I learn today?

Asr Afternoon
Prayer

Maghrib Sunset
Prayer & Iftar Meal

HEART CHECK-IN		SALAH	
Dua		Fajr	
Dhikr		Dhuhr	
Quran		Asr	
Charity		Maghrib	
Tarawih		Isha	

**IMPORTANT TASKS
FOR TODAY**

1)

2)

3)

**GOOD DEEDS
FOR TODAY**

1)

2)

3)

**IMPORTANT TASKS
FOR TOMORROW**

1)

2)

3)

Let's recite the Ayat al-Kursi.

Ubayy ibn Ka'b reported: The Messenger of Allah, peace and blessings be upon him, said: "O Abu Mundhir, do you know which verse in the book of Allah is greatest?" I recited the verse of the throne: "Allah, there is no God but Him, the Living, the Sustainer" (2:255). The Prophet struck me on the chest and said, "By Allah, O Abu Mundhir, rejoice in this knowledge!" When should one recite *Ayat al-Kursi*? It is a protection and means to be uplifted at any time, but we are particularly recommended to recite it after every prayer and before sleeping. Abu Umamah reported: The Messenger of Allah, peace and blessings be upon him, said: "Whoever recites the 'verse of the Throne' *(Ayat al-Kursi)* after every prescribed prayer will have nothing standing between him and his entry into Paradise but death."

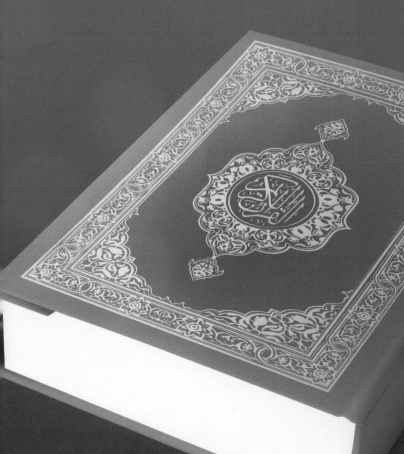

Scan to listen to Ayat al-Kursi.

www.ramadanrevival.co/moment2

RAMADAN

Did I fast?

Sahoor
Pre-dawn Meal

> *Our Lord, let not our hearts deviate after You have guided us and grant us from Yourself mercy. Indeed, You are the Bestower. (3:8)*

Fajr Dawn
Prayer

I am thankful for...

Dhuhr Noon
Prayer

Quran: What did I read today?

Asr Afternoon
Prayer

Quran: What did I learn today?

Maghrib Sunset
Prayer & Iftar Meal

HEART CHECK-IN		SALAH	
	Dua		Fajr
	Dhikr		Dhuhr
	Quran		Asr
	Charity		Maghrib
	Tarawih		Isha

IMPORTANT TASKS
FOR TODAY

1)

2)

3)

GOOD DEEDS
FOR TODAY

1)

2)

3)

IMPORTANT TASKS
FOR TOMORROW

1)

2)

3)

Duas
TO MAKE

Daily
REFLECTIONS

RAMADAN

Did I fast?

Sahoor
Pre-dawn Meal

> *Our Lord, forgive us our sins and the excess [committed] in our affairs and plant firmly our feet and give us victory over the disbelieving people. (3:147)*

Fajr Dawn
Prayer

I am thankful for...

Dhuhr Noon
Prayer

Quran: What did I read today?

Asr Afternoon
Prayer

Quran: What did I learn today?

Maghrib Sunset
Prayer & Iftar Meal

HEART CHECK-IN
- Dua
- Dhikr
- Quran
- Charity
- Tarawih

SALAH
- Fajr
- Dhuhr
- Asr
- Maghrib
- Isha

**IMPORTANT TASKS
FOR TODAY**

1)

_____

2)

_____

3)

Duas TO MAKE

**GOOD DEEDS
FOR TODAY**

1)

_____

2)

_____

3)

Daily REFLECTIONS

**IMPORTANT TASKS
FOR TOMORROW**

1)

_____

2)

_____

3)

08

RAMADAN

DATE

Did I fast?

Sahoor
Pre-dawn Meal

> *Our Lord, indeed whoever You admit to the Fire - You have disgraced him, and for the wrongdoers there are no helpers. (3:192)*

Fajr Dawn
Prayer

I am thankful for...

Dhuhr Noon
Prayer

Quran: What did I read today?

Asr Afternoon
Prayer

Quran: What did I learn today?

Maghrib Sunset
Prayer & Iftar Meal

HEART CHECK-IN
- Dua
- Dhikr
- Quran
- Charity
- Tarawih

SALAH
- Fajr
- Dhuhr
- Asr
- Maghrib
- Isha

**IMPORTANT TASKS
FOR TODAY**

1)
_____

2)
_____

3)

**GOOD DEEDS
FOR TODAY**

1)
_____

2)
_____

3)

Daily
REFLECTIONS

**IMPORTANT TASKS
FOR TOMORROW**

1)
_____

2)
_____

3)

A MOMENT WITH THE MESSENGER ﷺ

SCAN ME

Scan to watch.
www.ramadanrevival.co/moment3

RAMADAN

Did I fast?

Sahoor
Pre-dawn Meal

....

....

....

> Our Lord, indeed we have heard a caller calling to faith, [saying], 'Believe in your Lord,' and we have believed. (3:193)

Fajr Dawn
Prayer

....

....

....

I am thankful for...

Dhuhr Noon
Prayer

....

....

Quran: What did I read today?

Asr Afternoon
Prayer

....

....

....

Quran: What did I learn today?

Maghrib Sunset
Prayer & Iftar Meal

....

....

HEART CHECK-IN		SALAH	
Dua		Fajr	
Dhikr		Dhuhr	
Quran		Asr	
Charity		Maghrib	
Tarawih		Isha	

**IMPORTANT TASKS
FOR TODAY**

1)

2)

3)

**GOOD DEEDS
FOR TODAY**

1)

2)

3)

**IMPORTANT TASKS
FOR TOMORROW**

1)

2)

3)

Duas
TO MAKE

Daily
REFLECTIONS

RAMADAN

Did I fast?

Sahoor
Pre-dawn Meal

> *Our Lord, forgive us our sins and remove from us our misdeeds and cause us to die with the righteous. (3:193)*

Fajr Dawn
Prayer

I am thankful for...

Dhuhr Noon
Prayer

Quran: What did I read today?

Asr Afternoon
Prayer

Quran: What did I learn today?

Maghrib Sunset
Prayer & Iftar Meal

HEART CHECK-IN
- Dua
- Dhikr
- Quran
- Charity
- Tarawih

SALAH
- Fajr
- Dhuhr
- Asr
- Maghrib
- Isha

IMPORTANT TASKS
FOR TODAY

1)

2)

3)

GOOD DEEDS
FOR TODAY

1)

2)

3)

IMPORTANT TASKS
FOR TOMORROW

1)

2)

3)

Duas
TO MAKE

Daily
REFLECTIONS

RAMADAN
RECAP
MOMENT

Scan to watch.
www.ramadanrevival.co/moment4

RAMADAN

Did I fast?

Sahoor
Pre-dawn Meal

> *Our Lord, and grant us what You promised us through Your messengers and do not disgrace us on the Day of Resurrection. Indeed, You do not fail in [Your] promise. (3:193)*

Fajr Dawn
Prayer

I am thankful for...

Dhuhr Noon
Prayer

Quran: What did I read today?

Asr Afternoon
Prayer

Quran: What did I learn today?

Maghrib Sunset
Prayer & Iftar Meal

HEART CHECK-IN		SALAH	
Dua		Fajr	
Dhikr		Dhuhr	
Quran		Asr	
Charity		Maghrib	
Tarawih		Isha	

IMPORTANT TASKS FOR TODAY

1)

2)

3)

GOOD DEEDS FOR TODAY

1)

2)

3)

IMPORTANT TASKS FOR TOMORROW

1)

2)

3)

RAMADAN

Did I fast?

Sahoor
Pre-dawn Meal

....

....

....

Fajr Dawn
Prayer

....

....

....

....

Dhuhr Noon
Prayer

....

....

....

Asr Afternoon
Prayer

....

....

....

....

Maghrib Sunset
Prayer & Iftar Meal

....

....

> *Our Lord, we have wronged ourselves, and if You do not forgive us and have mercy upon us, we will surely be among the losers. (7:23)*

I am thankful for...

Quran: What did I read today?

Quran: What did I learn today?

HEART CHECK-IN		SALAH	
Dua		Fajr	
Dhikr		Dhuhr	
Quran		Asr	
Charity		Maghrib	
Tarawih		Isha	

IMPORTANT TASKS
FOR TODAY

1)

2)

3)

GOOD DEEDS
FOR TODAY

1)

2)

3)

IMPORTANT TASKS
FOR TOMORROW

1)

2)

3)

RAMADAN

Did I fast?

Sahoor
Pre-dawn Meal

> *Our Lord, do not place us with the
> wrongdoing people. (7:47)*

Fajr Dawn
Prayer

I am thankful for...

Dhuhr Noon
Prayer

Quran: What did I read today?

Quran: What did I learn today?

Asr Afternoon
Prayer

Maghrib Sunset
Prayer & Iftar Meal

HEART CHECK-IN
- Dua
- Dhikr
- Quran
- Charity
- Tarawih

SALAH
- Fajr
- Dhuhr
- Asr
- Maghrib
- Isha

**IMPORTANT TASKS
FOR TODAY**

1)
_____

2)
_____

3)
_____

**GOOD DEEDS
FOR TODAY**

1)
_____

2)
_____

3)
_____

**IMPORTANT TASKS
FOR TOMORROW**

1)
_____

2)
_____

3)
_____

Duas
TO MAKE

Daily
REFLECTIONS

RAMADAN

Did I fast?

Sahoor
Pre-dawn Meal

> *Our Lord, decide between us and our people in truth, and You are the best of those who give decision. (7:89)*

Fajr Dawn
Prayer

I am thankful for...

Dhuhr Noon
Prayer

Quran: What did I read today?

Asr Afternoon
Prayer

Quran: What did I learn today?

Maghrib Sunset
Prayer & Iftar Meal

HEART CHECK-IN
- Dua
- Dhikr
- Quran
- Charity
- Tarawih

SALAH
- Fajr
- Dhuhr
- Asr
- Maghrib
- Isha

**IMPORTANT TASKS
FOR TODAY**

Duas
TO MAKE

1)

2)

3)

**GOOD DEEDS
FOR TODAY**

1)

2)

Daily
REFLECTIONS

3)

**IMPORTANT TASKS
FOR TOMORROW**

1)

2)

3)

A MOMENT
WITH THE
MESSENGER ﷺ

Salawat — Start with 10 but aim for 100.

Allahumma salli 'ala Muhammadin wa 'ala ali Muhammad(in), kama sallayta 'ala Ibrahima wa 'ala ali Ibrahim(a), innaka Hamidun Majid. Allahumma barik 'ala Muhammadin wa 'ala ali Muhammad(in), kama barakta 'ala Ibrahima wa 'ala ali Ibrahim(a), innaka Hamidun Majid.

O Allah, send prayers upon Muhammad and upon the family of Muhammad just as You have sent prayers upon Ibrahim and upon the family of Ibrahim, verily You are the Praiseworthy, the Glorious. O Allah, bless Muhammad and the family of Muhammad just as You have blessed Ibrahim and the family of Ibrahim, verily You are the Praiseworthy, the Glorious.

اللَّهُمَّ صَلِّ عَلَى مُحَمَّدٍ وَعَلَى آلِ مُحَمَّدٍ كَمَا صَلَّيْتَ عَلَى إِبْرَاهِيمَ وَعَلَى آلِ إِبْرَاهِيمَ إِنَّكَ حَمِيدٌ مَجِيدٌ اللَّهُمَّ بَارِكْ عَلَى مُحَمَّدٍ وَعَلَى آلِ مُحَمَّدٍ كَمَا بَارَكْتَ عَلَى إِبْرَاهِيمَ وَعَلَى آلِ إِبْرَاهِيمَ إِنَّكَ حَمِيدٌ مَجِيدٌ

RAMADAN

15

Did I fast?

Sahoor
Pre-dawn Meal

> *Our Lord, pour upon us patience and let us die as Muslims [in submission to You]. (7:126)*

Fajr Dawn
Prayer

I am thankful for...

Dhuhr Noon
Prayer

Quran: What did I read today?

Asr Afternoon
Prayer

Quran: What did I learn today?

Maghrib Sunset
Prayer & Iftar Meal

HEART CHECK-IN

- Dua
- Dhikr
- Quran
- Charity
- Tarawih

SALAH

- Fajr
- Dhuhr
- Asr
- Maghrib
- Isha

**IMPORTANT TASKS
FOR TODAY**

1)

2)

3)

**GOOD DEEDS
FOR TODAY**

1)

2)

3)

**IMPORTANT TASKS
FOR TOMORROW**

1)

2)

3)

Duas
TO MAKE

Daily
REFLECTIONS

16

RAMADAN

Did I fast?

Sahoor
Pre-dawn Meal

....

....

....

> *Our Lord, make us not [objects of] trial for the wrongdoing people; And save us by Your mercy from the disbelieving people. (10:85-86)*

Fajr Dawn
Prayer

I am thankful for...

....

....

....

....

Dhuhr Noon
Prayer

Quran: What did I read today?

....

....

....

Asr Afternoon
Prayer

Quran: What did I learn today?

....

....

....

....

....

Maghrib Sunset
Prayer & Iftar Meal

HEART CHECK-IN		SALAH	
Dua		Fajr	
Dhikr		Dhuhr	
Quran		Asr	
Charity		Maghrib	
Tarawih		Isha	

....

....

IMPORTANT TASKS
FOR TODAY

1)

2)

3)

GOOD DEEDS
FOR TODAY

1)

2)

3)

IMPORTANT TASKS
FOR TOMORROW

1)

2)

3)

RAMADAN

Did I fast?

Sahoor
Pre-dawn Meal

....

....

....

> Our Lord, indeed You know what we conceal and what we declare, and nothing is hidden from Allah on the earth or in the heaven. (14:38)

Fajr Dawn
Prayer

I am thankful for...

....

....

....

Dhuhr Noon
Prayer

Quran: What did I read today?

....

....

....

Quran: What did I learn today?

Asr Afternoon
Prayer

....

....

....

Maghrib Sunset
Prayer & Iftar Meal

....

....

....

HEART CHECK-IN		SALAH	
Dua		Fajr	
Dhikr		Dhuhr	
Quran		Asr	
Charity		Maghrib	
Tarawih		Isha	

**IMPORTANT TASKS
FOR TODAY**

Duas
TO MAKE

1)

2)

3)

**GOOD DEEDS
FOR TODAY**

1)

2)

Daily
REFLECTIONS

3)

**IMPORTANT TASKS
FOR TOMORROW**

1)

2)

3)

QURAN

Let's recite Surah Ya Sin.

Scan to watch.

www.ramadanrevival.co/moment6

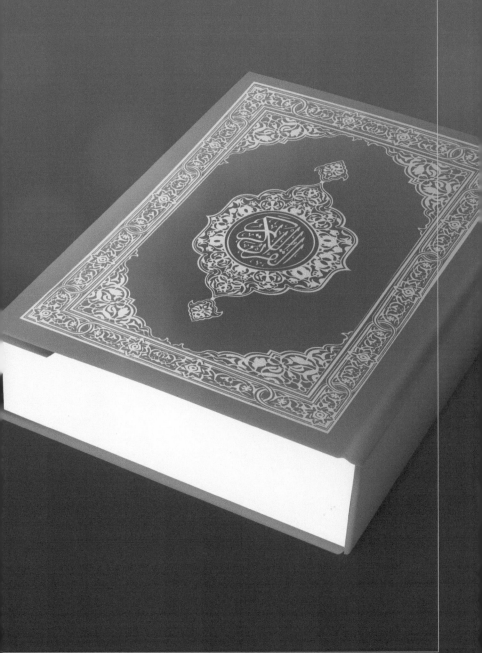

RAMADAN

Did I fast?

Sahoor
Pre-dawn Meal

> *Our Lord, grant us from Yourself mercy and prepare for us from our affair right guidance. (18:10)*

Fajr Dawn
Prayer

I am thankful for...

Quran: What did I read today?

Dhuhr Noon
Prayer

Quran: What did I learn today?

Asr Afternoon
Prayer

HEART CHECK-IN		SALAH	
Dua		Fajr	
Dhikr		Dhuhr	
Quran		Asr	
Charity		Maghrib	
Tarawih		Isha	

Maghrib Sunset
Prayer & Iftar Meal

**IMPORTANT TASKS
FOR TODAY**

1)

2)

3)

**GOOD DEEDS
FOR TODAY**

1)

2)

3)

**IMPORTANT TASKS
FOR TOMORROW**

1)

2)

3)

Duas
TO MAKE

Daily
REFLECTIONS

RAMADAN

Did I fast?

Sahoor
Pre-dawn Meal

> *Oh Allah, bless the person in my lineage who first converted to Islam.*

Fajr Dawn
Prayer

I am thankful for...

Quran: What did I read today?

Dhuhr Noon
Prayer

Quran: What did I learn today?

Asr Afternoon
Prayer

Maghrib Sunset
Prayer & Iftar Meal

HEART CHECK-IN		SALAH	
	Dua		Fajr
	Dhikr		Dhuhr
	Quran		Asr
	Charity		Maghrib
	Tarawih		Isha

IMPORTANT TASKS
FOR TODAY

1)

_____

2)

_____

3)

_____

GOOD DEEDS
FOR TODAY

1)

_____

2)

_____

3)

_____

IMPORTANT TASKS
FOR TOMORROW

1)

_____

2)

_____

3)

_____

RAMADAN
RECAP
MOMENT

Scan to watch.
www.ramadanrevival.co/moment10

DATE

Did I fast?

Sahoor
Pre-dawn Meal

....

....

....

> *Our Lord, You have encompassed all things in mercy and knowledge, so forgive those who have repented and followed Your way and protect them from the punishment of Hellfire. (40:7)*

Fajr Dawn
Prayer

....

....

....

I am thankful for...

Dhuhr Noon
Prayer

....

....

....

Quran: What did I read today?

Asr Afternoon
Prayer

....

....

....

Quran: What did I learn today?

Maghrib Sunset
Prayer & Iftar Meal

....

....

HEART CHECK-IN	SALAH
Dua	Fajr
Dhikr	Dhuhr
Quran	Asr
Charity	Maghrib
Tarawih	Isha

**IMPORTANT TASKS
FOR TODAY**

1)

2)

3)

Duas
TO MAKE

**GOOD DEEDS
FOR TODAY**

1)

2)

3)

Daily
REFLECTIONS

**IMPORTANT TASKS
FOR TOMORROW**

1)

2)

3)

DHIKR

Astaghfirullah (99 times)

I seek God's forgiveness

MOMENT

أَسْتَغْفِرُ ٱللّٰه

RAMADAN

Did I fast?

Sahoor
Pre-dawn Meal

....

....

....

> O Allah, I seek Your forgiveness and my well-being in this world and the Hereafter (Sunan Ibn Majah).

Fajr Dawn
Prayer

....

....

....

I am thankful for...

Dhuhr Noon
Prayer

....

....

....

Quran: What did I read today?

Asr Afternoon
Prayer

....

....

....

....

....

Quran: What did I learn today?

Maghrib Sunset
Prayer & Iftar Meal

....

....

....

HEART CHECK-IN

- Dua
- Dhikr
- Quran
- Charity
- Tarawih

SALAH

- Fajr
- Dhuhr
- Asr
- Maghrib
- Isha

**IMPORTANT TASKS
FOR TODAY**

1)

2)

3)

**GOOD DEEDS
FOR TODAY**

1)

2)

3)

**IMPORTANT TASKS
FOR TOMORROW**

1)

2)

3)

RAMADAN

Did I fast?

Sahoor
Pre-dawn Meal

> *O Allah protect me from my front, behind me, my right and my left, from above me, and I seek refuge in Your Magnificence from being taken unaware from beneath me (Sunan Ibn Majah).*

Fajr Dawn
Prayer

I am thankful for...

Dhuhr Noon
Prayer

Quran: What did I read today?

Asr Afternoon
Prayer

Quran: What did I learn today?

Maghrib Sunset
Prayer & Iftar Meal

HEART CHECK-IN		SALAH	
Dua		Fajr	
Dhikr		Dhuhr	
Quran		Asr	
Charity		Maghrib	
Tarawih		Isha	

IMPORTANT TASKS
FOR TODAY

1)
_____

2)
_____

3)
_____

GOOD DEEDS
FOR TODAY

1)
_____

2)
_____

3)
_____

IMPORTANT TASKS
FOR TOMORROW

1)
_____

2)
_____

3)
_____

Duas
TO MAKE

Daily
REFLECTIONS

DHIKR

Astaghfirullah (99 times)

I seek God's forgiveness

MOMENT

أَسْتَغْفِرُ ٱللَّه

DATE

Did I fast?

Sahoor
Pre-dawn Meal

....
....
....

> Our Lord, forgive us and our brothers who preceded us in faith and put not in our hearts [any] resentment toward those who have believed. Our Lord, indeed You are Kind and Merciful." (59:10)

Fajr Dawn
Prayer

....
....
....
....
....

I am thankful for...

Dhuhr Noon
Prayer

....
....
....

Quran: What did I read today?

Asr Afternoon
Prayer

....
....
....
....
....

Quran: What did I learn today?

Maghrib Sunset
Prayer & Iftar Meal

....
....

HEART CHECK-IN

- Dua
- Dhikr
- Quran
- Charity
- Tarawih

SALAH

- Fajr
- Dhuhr
- Asr
- Maghrib
- Isha

IMPORTANT TASKS
FOR TODAY

1)

2)

3)

GOOD DEEDS
FOR TODAY

1)

2)

3)

IMPORTANT TASKS
FOR TOMORROW

1)

2)

3)

Duas
TO MAKE

Daily
REFLECTIONS

RAMADAN

Did I fast?

Sahoor
Pre-dawn Meal

....

....

....

> *Our Lord, upon You we have relied, and to You we have returned, and to You is the destination. (60:4)*

Fajr Dawn
Prayer

I am thankful for...

....

....

....

....

Dhuhr Noon
Prayer

Quran: What did I read today?

....

....

....

Asr Afternoon
Prayer

Quran: What did I learn today?

....

....

....

....

....

Maghrib Sunset
Prayer & Iftar Meal

....

....

....

HEART CHECK-IN		SALAH	
Dua		Fajr	
Dhikr		Dhuhr	
Quran		Asr	
Charity		Maghrib	
Tarawih		Isha	

IMPORTANT TASKS
FOR TODAY

1)

2)

3)

GOOD DEEDS
FOR TODAY

1)

2)

3)

IMPORTANT TASKS
FOR TOMORROW

1)

2)

3)

Duas
TO MAKE

Daily
REFLECTIONS

DHIKR

Astaghfirullah (99 times)

I seek God's forgiveness

أَسْتَغْفِرُ ٱللَّه

RAMADAN

Did I fast?

Sahoor
Pre-dawn Meal

....
....
....

> *Our Lord, perfect for us our light and forgive us.*
> *Indeed, You are over all things competent. (66:8)*

Fajr Dawn
Prayer

....
....
....

I am thankful for...

Dhuhr Noon
Prayer

....
....
....

Quran: What did I read today?

Asr Afternoon
Prayer

....
....
....

Quran: What did I learn today?

Maghrib Sunset
Prayer & Iftar Meal

....
....

HEART CHECK-IN
- Dua
- Dhikr
- Quran
- Charity
- Tarawih

SALAH
- Fajr
- Dhuhr
- Asr
- Maghrib
- Isha

IMPORTANT TASKS
FOR TODAY

1)

2)

3)

GOOD DEEDS
FOR TODAY

1)

2)

3)

IMPORTANT TASKS
FOR TOMORROW

1)

2)

3)

Duas
TO MAKE

Daily
REFLECTIONS

RAMADAN

DATE

Did I fast?

Sahoor
Pre-dawn Meal

> *I seek protection in the perfect words of Allah from every evil that has been created (Sahih Muslim).*

Fajr Dawn
Prayer

I am thankful for...

Dhuhr Noon
Prayer

Quran: What did I read today?

Asr Afternoon
Prayer

Quran: What did I learn today?

Maghrib Sunset
Prayer & Iftar Meal

HEART CHECK-IN

Dua
Dhikr
Quran
Charity
Tarawih

SALAH

Fajr
Dhuhr
Asr
Maghrib
Isha

**IMPORTANT TASKS
FOR TODAY**

1)

2)

3)

**GOOD DEEDS
FOR TODAY**

1)

2)

3)

**IMPORTANT TASKS
FOR TOMORROW**

1)

2)

3)

Duas
TO MAKE

Daily
REFLECTIONS

Astaghfirullah (99 times)

I seek God's forgiveness

أَسْتَغْفِرُ ٱللَّه

RAMADAN

Did I fast?

Sahoor
Pre-dawn Meal

....

....

....

> ❝
>
> *There is no power or might
> except (by) Allah.*

Fajr Dawn
Prayer

I am thankful for...

....

....

....

....

Dhuhr Noon
Prayer

Quran: What did I read today?

....

....

....

Asr Afternoon
Prayer

Quran: What did I learn today?

....

....

....

....

Maghrib Sunset
Prayer & Iftar Meal

....

....

HEART CHECK-IN		SALAH	
	Dua		Fajr
	Dhikr		Dhuhr
	Quran		Asr
	Charity		Maghrib
	Tarawih		Isha

**IMPORTANT TASKS
FOR TODAY**

1)

2)

3)

**GOOD DEEDS
FOR TODAY**

1)

2)

3)

**IMPORTANT TASKS
FOR TOMORROW**

1)

2)

3)

RAMADAN

Did I fast?

Sahoor
Pre-dawn Meal

....

....

....

> *All praise is for Allah.*

Fajr Dawn
Prayer

....

....

....

I am thankful for...

Dhuhr Noon
Prayer

....

....

....

Quran: What did I read today?

Asr Afternoon
Prayer

....

....

....

....

Quran: What did I learn today?

Maghrib Sunset
Prayer & Iftar Meal

....

....

....

HEART CHECK-IN
- Dua
- Dhikr
- Quran
- Charity
- Tarawih

SALAH
- Fajr
- Dhuhr
- Asr
- Maghrib
- Isha

IMPORTANT TASKS
FOR TODAY

1)

2)

3)

GOOD DEEDS
FOR TODAY

1)

2)

3)

IMPORTANT TASKS
FOR TOMORROW

1)

2)

3)

Duas
TO MAKE

Daily
REFLECTIONS

RAMADAN
RECAP
MOMENT

Scan to watch.
www.ramadanrevival.co/moment11

RAMADAN

Did I fast?

Sahoor
Pre-dawn Meal

> *Exalted is Allah.*

Fajr Dawn
Prayer

I am thankful for...

Quran: What did I read today?

Dhuhr Noon
Prayer

Quran: What did I learn today?

Asr Afternoon
Prayer

HEART CHECK-IN
- Dua
- Dhikr
- Quran
- Charity
- Tarawih

SALAH
- Fajr
- Dhuhr
- Asr
- Maghrib
- Isha

Maghrib Sunset
Prayer & Iftar Meal

IMPORTANT TASKS
FOR TODAY

1)

2)

3)

GOOD DEEDS
FOR TODAY

1)

2)

3)

IMPORTANT TASKS
FOR TOMORROW

1)

2)

3)

Duas
TO MAKE

Daily
REFLECTIONS

RAMADAN

Did I fast?

Sahoor
Pre-dawn Meal

> *Oh Allah, bless my mother and father.*

Fajr Dawn
Prayer

I am thankful for...

Quran: What did I read today?

Dhuhr Noon
Prayer

Quran: What did I learn today?

Asr Afternoon
Prayer

Maghrib Sunset
Prayer & Iftar Meal

HEART CHECK-IN
- Dua
- Dhikr
- Quran
- Charity
- Tarawih

SALAH
- Fajr
- Dhuhr
- Asr
- Maghrib
- Isha

IMPORTANT TASKS
FOR TODAY

1)

2)

3)

GOOD DEEDS
FOR TODAY

1)

2)

3)

IMPORTANT TASKS
FOR TOMORROW

1)

2)

3)

Duas
TO MAKE

Daily
REFLECTIONS

MY PRAYERS

Use this section to gather your prayers
to recite throughout Ramadan.

My Lord,

_____

_____

_____

_____

_____

_____

_____

_____

_____

_____

_____

_____

_____

_____

FINAL THOUGHTS

Use this section to reflect on your
Ramadan experience.